John Taven[er]
Christmas
Choral Collection

Chester Music
part of The Music Sales Group
14-15 Berners Street, London W1T 3LJ

CHESTER MUSIC

COMPOSER'S NOTES

Introduction

The Orthodox concept of Christmas is above all one of The Incarnation of the Logos (The Word made Flesh). It is perhaps the most magnificent and awesome event of all time.

Carols in the Orthodox East are sung *after* Christmas. There is no advent, as such, just a period of fasting, which is broken on Christmas Day. Most of the words in this book are from Orthodox texts: from the Eve of Christmas, the canons before this, or from Christmas Day itself.

None of them makes any sentimental comment on the child, Jesus. As in ikons He is represented as *puer senex* (boy/old man). Because of the vast and magnificent event of The Incarnation of the Logos we are all invited, or commanded, to become Christ, and that is what the Saints are – Christ, but in another form. Such is the awesome message of the Incarnation: "God is with us, understand ye nations, for God is with us."

1. God Is With Us

Commissioned for Winchester Cathedral with the generous support of Mr Jonathan Louth, in tribute to Martin Neary for his work at Winchester Cathedral during the years 1972–1987. First performance on 22nd December 1987 by the Choir of Winchester Cathedral, conducted by Martin Neary.

Text adapted from the Orthodox Great Compline for Christmas Eve.

2. Today The Virgin

First performance on 27th December 1989 at Westminster Abbey, London, by the Choir of Westminster Abbey conducted by Martin Neary.

Words by Mother Thekla.

3. The Lamb

First performance by the Choir of King's College, Cambridge, conducted by Stephen Cleobury, as part of A Festival of Nine Lessons and Carols on 24th December 1982.

Words by William Blake.

4. Ikon Of The Nativity

First performance on 20th December 1991 at the Henry Wood Hall, Glasgow, by Cappella Nova conducted by Alan Tavener.

Text by St Ephrem the Syrian
translated by Sebastian Brock.

Text is here set to music and reproduced by kind permission of Dr Sebastian Brock and the Fellowship of St Alban and St Sergius.

Praise to you to whom all things are easy, you are almighty.

St Ephrem the Syrian

Ikon Of The Nativity was written for Cappella Nova. The text is from a poem by the fourth century Syriac poet St Ephrem the Syrian, certainly the greatest poet of the Patristic age. He uses paradox to describe the indescribable, and could aptly be called the poet of Christian paradox.

This short piece concentrates on the Christian paradox. Indeed, Christ's presence in Mary's womb has the same effect as his presence in the bread and wine at the Eucharist. St Ephrem said "Fire and Spirit are in the womb of her who bore you..." and then he disarms the critic who would see his imagery as far-fetched when he says "This Jesus has made so many symbols that I have fallen into a sea of them."

5. O, Do Not Move
a miniature Ikon of the Nativity

First performance on 6th June 1992, at St John's, Smith Square, London, by the Holst Singers conducted by Nicholas Cleobury.

Words by Seferis
translated from the Greek by Philip Sherrard.
The text is set to music and reproduced by kind permission of Mrs Maro Seferis.

This work is dedicated to my longest and dearest friend, Dr Penny Turton. Like *Ikon Of The Nativity*, it follows the theme of double meanings; Seferis liked his poetry to be interpreted in more than one way.

6. Apolytikion of the Incarnation

Written in memory of Roger Gaunt, founder of the St Endellion Festival. First performance on 5th August 1998, by the St Endellion Chorus conducted by Richard Hickox.

Text from the Orthodox Services for Christmas.

If wished, the work may be performed antiphonally.

7. A Nativity

First performance in December 1987 at St Martin-in-the-Fields, London, by Haberdasher Aske's Girls' School Choir.

Words by W.B. Yeats.
Here set to music by kind permission of Michael and Anne Yeats.

8. A Christmas Round

First performance on 6th June 1992, at St John's, Smith Square, London, by the Holst Singers conducted by Nicholas Cleobury.

Text from the Orthodox Liturgy for Christmas Day.

J.T.

Order No. CH 61598
This collection © Copyright 1999 Chester Music Ltd.

Cover design by Michael Bell Design
Photograph by Guy Hills
Music processing:
    Nos. 1, 2, 3, 6, 7, 8 by Music Publishing Services
    Nos. 4 & 5 by Music Copying Services (South Wales)

for Martin Neary

GOD IS WITH US

for solo tenor, choir and organ

John Tavener

CH 61598

Declaim freely, in Byzantine style

† ✗ denotes a microtone, a characteristic 'break in the voice' of Byzantine chant
* Breathe when necessary, but not simultaneously.
** The soloist should sing from a different point, away from the main body of the choir.

4

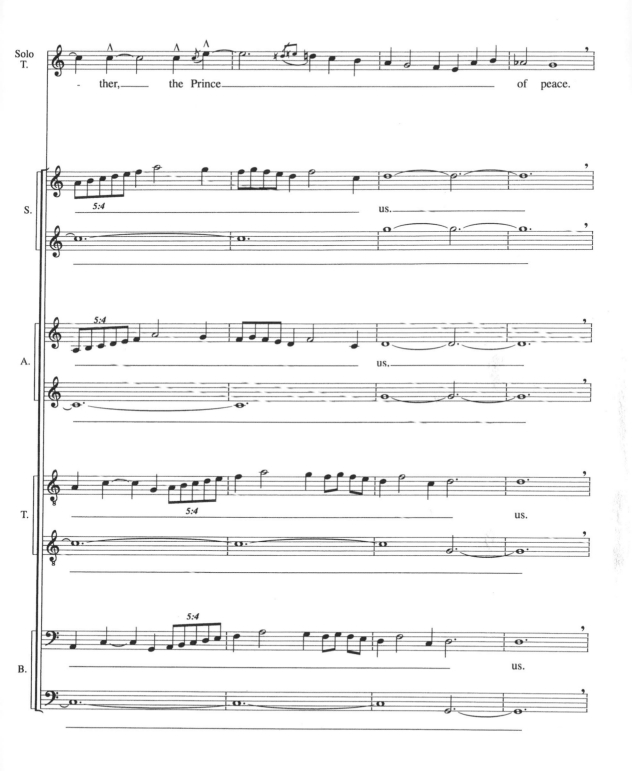

5

6

Sing 3 times: 1st time *f* > *mf*
            2nd time *mf* > *mp*
            3rd time *mp* > *p*

S. Hear____ ye peo - - - - ple, E - ven to the
A. Hear____ ye peo - - - - ple, E - ven to the
T. Hear____ ye peo - - - - ple, E - ven to the
B. Hear____ ye peo - - - - ple, E - ven to the

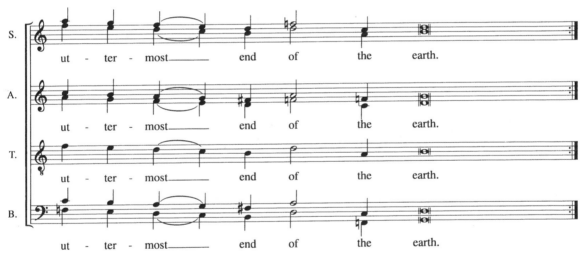

S. ut - ter - most____ end of the earth.
A. ut - ter - most____ end of the earth.
T. ut - ter - most____ end of the earth.
B. ut - ter - most____ end of the earth.

mf dolce
B. God____ is__ with____ us.
p sonore
Go(d).____

8

Katounia Limni
13th October 1987

TODAY THE VIRGIN

Mother Thekla

John Tavener

*'Oh' as in the 'o' of 'log'. Breathe when necessary, but not simultaneously.

T. 2. Ma-ry, my wife, O Ma-ry, my wife!— What— do— I see? I took you blame-less be-

B. Oh. —————

S. Re-joice, O World!

A. Re-joice, O World!

T. fore the Lord From the priests— of the Tem - ple. What— do— I see? Re-joice, O World!

B. (Oh.) ————————————— Re-joice, O World!

S. With the An-gels and the Shep-herds Give glo-ry to the Child! Al-le-lu - i - a!

A. With the An-gels and the Shep-herds Give glo-ry to the Child! Al-le-lu - i - a!

T. With the An-gels and the Shep-herds Give glo-ry to the Child! Al-le-lu - i - a!

B. With the An-gels and the Shep-herds Give glo-ry to the Child! Al-le-lu - i - a!

S. 3. Jo-seph, the Bride-groom, O Jo-seph, the Bride-groom! Do__ not__ fear. God in His mer-cy has

A. Oh.

T. Oh.

S. come down to earth, He takes__ flesh in my womb For_ all the world_ to see. Re-joice, O World! With the

A. (Oh.)__ Re-joice, O World! With the

T. (Oh.)__ Re-joice, O World! With the

B. Re-joice, O World! With the

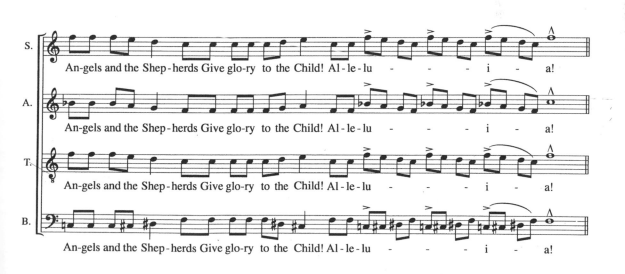

S. An-gels and the Shep-herds Give glo-ry to the Child! Al-le-lu - - i - a!

A. An-gels and the Shep-herds Give glo-ry to the Child! Al-le-lu - - i - a!

T. An-gels and the Shep-herds Give glo-ry to the Child! Al-le-lu - - i - a!

B. An-gels and the Shep-herds Give glo-ry to the Child! Al-le-lu - - i - a!

12

13

14

22nd September, 1989

for Simon's 3rd birthday

THE LAMB

William Blake

John Tavener

16

for Cappella Nova

IKON OF THE NATIVITY

St. Ephrem the Syrian

John Tavener

* 'Oh' as in the 'o' of 'log'. Breathe when necessary, but not simultaneously.

20

who can hope to____ un - der - stand____ Yours?

(Oh.)____

(Oh.)____

who can hope to____ un - der - stand____ Yours?

With Byzantine splendour, alternating with tenderness

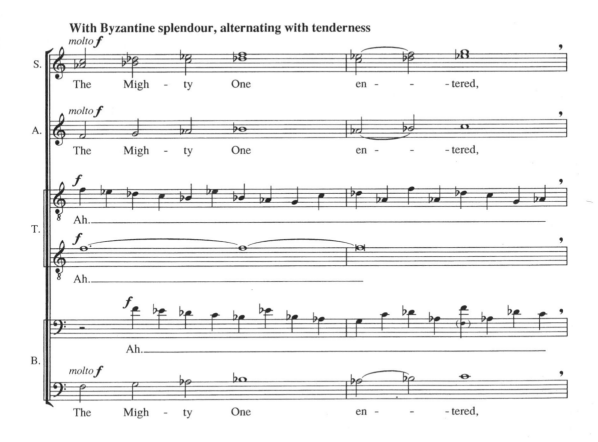

The Migh - ty One en - - -tered,

The Migh - ty One en - - -tered,

Ah.____

Ah.____

Ah.____

The Migh - ty One en - - -tered,

22

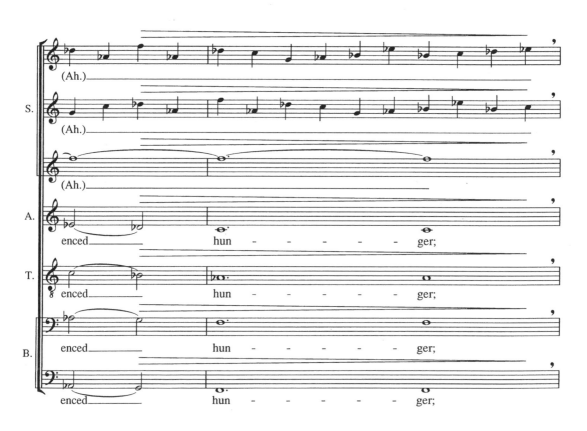

With Byzantine splendour

He who gives drink to all

He who gives drink to all

He who gives drink to all

Ah.

Ah.

Ah.

tenderly

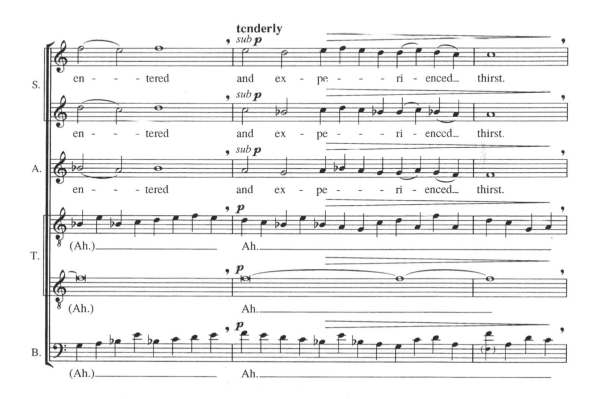

en - - tered and ex - pe - - - ri - enced thirst.

en - - tered and ex - pe - - - ri - enced thirst.

en - - tered and ex - pe - - - ri - enced thirst.

(Ah.) Ah.

(Ah.) Ah.

(Ah.) Ah.

24

massive

26

Sing 3 times
1st. time **mp**
2nd. time **p**
3rd. time **pp**

S. Praise to you to — whom all — things are — ea — — — sy,

A. Oh. —

T. Oh. —

B. Praise to you to — whom all — things are — ea — — — sy,

Pause last
time only

S. You are al - migh — — — — — — — — ty.

A. (Oh.) —

T. (Oh.) —

B. You are al - migh — — — — — — — — ty.

9th October 1991

for Penny

O, DO NOT MOVE

a miniature Ikon of the Nativity

Seferis

John Tavener

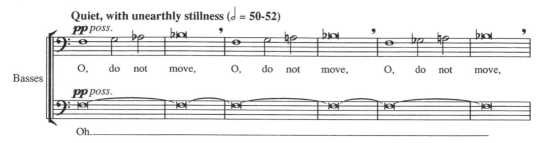

Nafsika, 9th November 1990

for the St. Endellion Festival

APOLYTIKION OF THE INCARNATION

John Tavener

* 'Oh' as in the 'o' of 'log'. Breathe when necessary, but not simultaneously.

† ⚡ represents a microtone, a characteristic 'break in the voice' of Byzantine chant.

33

36

Pigadaki
Christmas 1997

for Liadain Sherrard

A NATIVITY

for unaccompanied choir (SSSAA)

William Butler Yeats

John Tavener

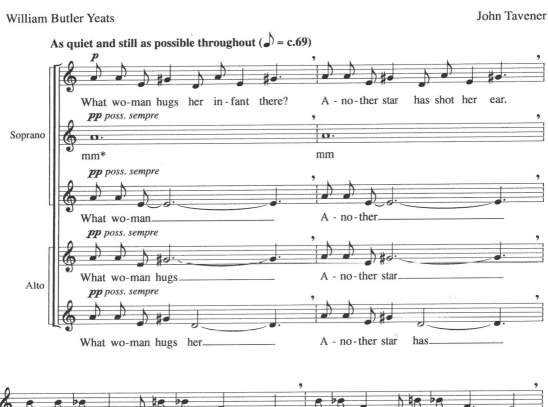

*hum with lips closed

What made the ceil - ing wa - ter - proof? Lan-dor's tar - pau - lin on the roof.

S. mm mm

What made the___ Lan-dor's tar___

A. What made the ceil___ Lan-dor's tar - pau___

What made the ceil - ing___ Lan-dor's tar - pau - lin___

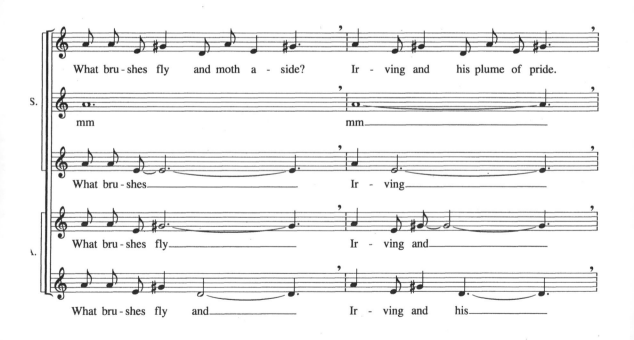

What bru - shes fly and moth a - side? Ir - ving and his plume of pride.

S. mm mm___

What bru - shes___ Ir - ving___

What bru - shes fly___ Ir - ving and___

What bru - shes fly and___ Ir - ving and his___

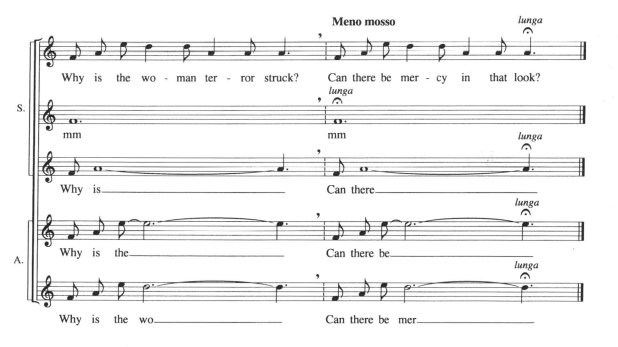

to Dimitri and Christina

A CHRISTMAS ROUND

John Tavener

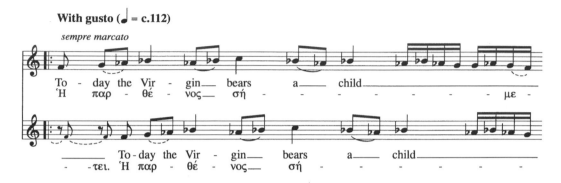

Feast of St. Nektarios of Aegina
9th November 1990

Performance Note

Any number of voices may perform this round, plus instruments (including unpitched percussion) if desired. A drone (on F) could also be added.

Transliteration of the Greek:

Ee parthénos séemeron ton eeperóosion tíktee.

10/12 (184790)